CH

NASA
ASTRONOMER
NANCY GRACE ROMAN

HEATHER E. SCHWARTZ

Lerner Publications • Minneapolis

Lerner Publications Company
A division of Lerner Publishing Group, Inc.
241 First Avenue North
Minneapolis, MN 55401 USA

For reading levels and more information, look up this title at www.lernerbooks.com.

Content Consultant: Liliya L.R. Williams, Professor, Minnesota Institute for Astrophysics

Library of Congress Cataloging-in-Publication Data

Names: Schwartz, Heather E.
Title: NASA astronomer Nancy Grace Roman / by Heather E. Schwartz.
Description: Minneapolis : Lerner Publications, [2018] | Series: STEM trailblazer bios | Audience: Age 7–11. | Audience: Grade 4 to 6. | Includes bibliographical references and index.
Identifiers: LCCN 2017011957 (print) | LCCN 2017016961 (ebook) | ISBN 9781512499858 (eb pdf) | ISBN 9781512499797 (lb : alk. paper)
Subjects: LCSH: Roman, Nancy Grace, 1925– | Women astronomers—United States—Biography—Juvenile literature. | Astronomers—United States—Biography—Juvenile literature. | United States. National Aeronautics and Space Administration—Officials and employees—Biography—Juvenile literature. | Hubble Space Telescope (Spacecraft)
Classification: LCC QB36.R738 (ebook) | LCC QB36.R738 S39 2018 (print) | DDC 520.92 [B] — dc23

LC record available at https://lccn.loc.gov/2017011957

Manufactured in the United States of America
1-43615-33366-5/16/2017

The images in this book are used with the permission of: © AIP Emilio Segre Visual Archives, Roman Collection, pp. 7, 16, 21, 27; Swarthmore College, p. 8; University of Chicago Library, Department of Special Collections, p. 10; Craig Ellenwood/Alamy Stock Photo, p. 11; Fredlyfish4/Shutterstock.com, p. 12; © iStockphoto.com/guvendemir, p. 14; NRAO/AUI/NSF, p. 15; © Bettmann/Getty Images, p. 18; NASA, pp. 20, 25; Photo Researchers, Inc/Alamy Stock Photo, p. 23; NASA-HUBBLE/age fotostock/Alamy Stock Photo, p. 26.

Front cover: © AIP Emilio Segre Visual Archives, Roman Collection.

Main body text set in Adrianna Regular 13/22. Typeface provided by Chank.

CONTENTS

Nancy Grace Roman worked on many projects at NASA, including the Orbiting Solar Observatory (*model pictured here*).

STARGAZING
STUDENT

Nancy Grace Roman always knew she wanted to be an **astronomer**. Most women of her time did not aim for scientific careers, but she didn't let that stop her. She studied astronomy and worked hard to prove herself. She even played a role in the development of an incredible piece of scientific equipment: the Hubble Space Telescope.

STUDYING THE STARS

Born in Nashville, Tennessee, in 1925, Nancy Grace moved many times throughout her childhood because of her father's job working for an oil company. Her father, Irwin Roman, was a geophysicist—a scientist that studies the physical processes that are going on in Earth. He often answered Nancy Grace's questions about science.

But it was her mother, Georgia Smith Roman, who inspired her passion for the stars. Her mother was not a scientist, but she was interested in the world around her. She took her daughter on nature walks, pointing out birds and plants. She showed Nancy Grace the **constellations** and the northern lights in the night sky.

When Nancy Grace was about eleven, the family moved to Reno, Nevada. There, she started her own neighborhood astronomy club. The girls in the club studied constellations and read about astronomy.

The Roman family moved to Baltimore, Maryland, in 1937, and Nancy Grace went to a girls' high school there. By then, she was already pursing her goal of becoming an astronomer.

TECH TALK

"I never seriously considered any occupation other than astronomy. A piece of artwork I did when I was in third grade shows a girl gazing out the window at the night sky, next to a poem about looking at the stars."

—*Nancy Grace Roman*

MOVING FORWARD

Nancy Grace had her parents' cautious support as she planned her path into the future. Her mother thought she should be open to studying other subjects too. She wanted her daughter to be happy. But she did not really believe science was the right field for a woman. Most women at that time did not pursue higher education. They married and had families instead.

Nancy Grace's high school guidance counselors seemed to feel the same way. They found her interest in science baffling. The only encouragement Nancy Grace found in high school was from one physics teacher who wanted to help. The problem was that the teacher didn't really know physics. The woman was a business education teacher who had been asked to take over the physics class.

Despite all of this, Nancy Grace worked hard to graduate from high school in three years instead of four. After high school, she chose to attend Swarthmore College in Pennsylvania. The school interested her for several reasons, but most important, the college had a strong astronomy program.

Nancy Grace (*back row, second from left*) with some of her schoolmates at Western High School in Baltimore, Maryland

Swarthmore College's newest observatory, the Peter van de Kamp Observatory, is named after one of Roman's teachers.

FINDING
HER WAY

In 1942, Roman started her first year at Swarthmore. She took history, German, math, and astronomy. Math and astronomy came naturally to her, while German and history were much more difficult. That confirmed her decision to keep moving toward her goal of becoming an astronomer.

Getting an education was challenging, however, even at a good school. Many teachers had left to help in World War II (1939–1945). Resources at the college were scarce too. The observatory, a special building with a telescope where astronomy students could study stars, planets, and galaxies, was in bad shape. Some locals were using the space to store onions, and the telescopes were old and not working well.

Still, Roman did not let difficult circumstances determine her future. She took matters into her own hands. She and another student took the telescopes in the observatory apart and cleaned their parts. They put the pieces together again and made adjustments so the telescopes would work better.

BUILDING A CAREER

After graduating from Swarthmore with a degree in astronomy, Roman continued her education. She decided to go to the University of Chicago's Yerkes Observatory in Williams Bay, Wisconsin. While she was there, she was most interested in **stellar astronomy**, the study of stars. She studied how stars move and how they are born, live, and die. She also enjoyed **spectral classification**, the sorting of stars based on their characteristics.

Roman (*front row, second from right*) and the Yerkes Observatory staff in 1946

May 1946

Roman earned her PhD in astronomy in 1949. After graduating, she worked for the university. For the first six years of her career, she was a research assistant and taught classes at Yerkes Observatory. She was the first woman on the academic staff there.

One project she worked on took her to the McDonald Observatory in West Texas. There, she examined stars by studying their light. She used a special tool to spread the light into a **spectrum**, or rainbow. Studying the spectrum allowed her to learn how fast stars were moving. It let her see how hot and bright the stars were. While Roman was at the McDonald Observatory, she noticed a strange star. It had been previously

Yerkes Observatory held the world's largest telescope when it first opened in 1897.

McDonald Observatory has many telescopes. This is the Hobby-Eberly Telescope.

classified as a star with characteristics very similar to the sun. But Roman found that the star was actually a completely different kind of star than what astronomers had previously thought. The star BD+67 922, later known as AG Draconis, became an important part of her research.

HITTING THE GLASS CEILING

Roman was excited by her work at the McDonald Observatory. She published a short piece about AG Draconis. Still, she could see she was limited at Yerkes Observatory. It was the 1950s, and her gender stood in her way.

There wasn't much opportunity then for a woman with Roman's education and talents to advance. She did not think she could get a good permanent position at the university. But she was intelligent, capable, and ambitious. She wanted to do more with her career.

TECH TALK

"My career was quite unusual so my main advice to someone interested in a career similar to my own is to remain open to change and new opportunities. I like to tell students that the jobs I took after my PhD were not in existence only a few years before."

—*Nancy Grace Roman*

Chapter 3

Roman made a name for herself doing groundbreaking research at the Naval Research Laboratory, including using radar to measure the distance to the moon.

JOINING NASA

Roman left Yerkes Observatory to work for the Naval Research Laboratory (NRL) in 1955. The lab conducts scientific research for the US Navy and US Marine Corps. At first, she had little to do. No one expected much from a female astronomer. So Roman worked on her own. Over time, she managed to gain acceptance from the group as they realized she could contribute to their work.

Her focus at the NRL was radio astronomy. She used radio waves to study space. The field was so new that radio astronomers had to build their own equipment. Roman did not enjoy that aspect of the work. She was an astronomer, not an engineer. But she still made several breakthroughs.

In 1930, Karl Guthe Jansky (*below*) built the now-famous merry-go-round structure that became the first radio wave detecting telescope (*also pictured below*).

Roman (*center*) developed a passion for teaching while giving her lectures. She would later become an advocate for women in the sciences.

Roman was among the first astronomers to determine the distance from Earth to the moon using radar measurements. She also received an invitation to spend time at the Soviet Academy of Sciences in the Soviet Union (a former nation made up of several modern-day countries, including Russia). The director of an observatory there was interested in the piece she had published about AG Draconis.

After working in the Soviet Union, Roman returned to the United States and gave a presentation on her trip. She was then asked to give a series of talks in an informal astronomy course for engineers and scientists. She enjoyed these talks because her audience was familiar enough with science basics that Roman was able to focus on more difficult astronomy concepts.

MOVING ON AND UP

Two years later, in 1958, the National Aeronautics and Space Administration (NASA) was formed. Much of the NRL's work was transferred there.

NASA AND THE SPACE RACE

In the 1950s, the United States was in a race with other nations to develop new technology and explore space. The main competition was the Soviet Union. That nation was the first to launch an artificial satellite into Earth's orbit when it sent the satellite *Sputnik* into space in 1957. In 1958, US president Dwight D. Eisenhower established NASA, an organization focused on researching flight in space and within Earth's **atmosphere**.

As NASA was growing, the organization needed someone to set up a space astronomy program. Roman considered the opportunity carefully and decided it was right for her.

Roman was hired as NASA's first Chief of Astronomy in 1959. This time, her gender became an asset. She was the first woman in a senior executive position at NASA, and the media took notice. Eager reporters featured Roman in parts

Roman stands near models of some of the projects she helped support. The small model in the foreground is an Advanced Orbiting Solar Observatory. The larger model is an Orbiting Astronomical Observatory.

TECH TALK

"When NASA was formed, one of the men there asked me if I knew anyone who would like to set up a program in space astronomy. And I decided that the idea of influencing astronomy for fifty years was just more than I could resist, and so I took the job."

—*Nancy Grace Roman*

of the paper devoted to news about and for women, giving her a lot of attention for her new position. It opened up more opportunities than she might have had otherwise.

In her new job, Roman reached out to the astronomy community. She visited astronomers and talked to them about NASA's plans for a program in space astronomy. She also listened. She wanted to know what they needed most from NASA as the program developed.

It turned out what astronomers wanted most was better, sharper images of their observations. Their desire led to Roman's work on the Hubble Space Telescope.

Chapter 4

The Hubble Space Telescope was the biggest project Roman worked on.

MOTHER OF
HUBBLE

Roman was on a mission. She wanted to help astronomers get better images from space. Earth's atmosphere distorts our view of space, making objects such as stars shimmer and move. This makes it very hard to take pictures of space from Earth through the atmosphere. A telescope in space wouldn't have the atmospheric interference. It wasn't a new idea. In 1946, a Yale professor named Lyman Spitzer Jr. had published a paper about putting a telescope in space. But the technology available then made it impossible. However, in the early 1960s, the idea could become a reality.

Roman started by creating a committee of astronomers from across the United States and engineers from NASA. The astronomers contributed ideas about what they wanted. The

Roman (*fifth from right*) worked with a committee of astronomers to determine what they needed from NASA.

engineers contributed thoughts about how to make those ideas work.

Next, Roman had to convince people that the telescope was worth building. She persuaded her bosses at NASA. She gave presentations to political leaders, explaining the scientific benefits that could be gained. It would help astronomers study stars, measure the distance from Earth to other galaxies, and learn about the physics of our universe.

The idea of a space telescope was exciting to many astronomers and engineers. But politicians were not so easily convinced. It was going to cost $400 to $500 million to build. Roman and her team worked to bring the cost down and eventually got the project approved.

BUILDING THE HUBBLE

The team finally began designing Hubble in 1978. NASA needed to build the telescope itself as well as the spacecraft to bring it into space.

In 1979, Roman retired from NASA. She kept up her work as an advocate for science. She visited schools and encouraged young girls to go into science. Meanwhile, the Hubble project she'd kicked off continued.

The Hubble Space Telescope was finally completed in 1984.

The Hubble Space Telescope received its finishing touches in 1984.

NAMING THE HUBBLE

In 1983, the Hubble Space Telescope was named after Edwin P. Hubble, an important astronomer during the 1920s. He made many discoveries. He proved that there are galaxies besides the Milky Way and that the universe is expanding.

It was about the size of a school bus. The spacecraft that was to take it to space was finished in 1985. Its launch was planned for 1986 but was delayed when the space shuttle *Challenger* exploded shortly after takeoff earlier that year. Hubble was finally launched into space aboard the *Discovery* in 1990.

HUBBLE'S CONTRIBUTIONS

Since then, Hubble has been capturing breathtaking images of space. After a NASA mission to adjust the telescope in 1993, the pictures sent back to Earth were some of the best scientists had ever seen.

Hubble orbits Earth, moving at a speed of about 5 miles (8 km) per second. It has captured incredible images of stars,

This Hubble
Space Telescope
image reveals a pair of
one-half-light-year-long
"twisters" that formed
between stars 5,000
light-years away.

The Hubble
Space Telescope
hovers at the
boundary of Earth
and space.

planets, comets, and galaxies trillions of miles away. The images are sent back to Earth through radio waves.

Astronomers have learned a lot about space from Hubble. The telescope has allowed them to see how planets and galaxies are formed. It has shown them evidence that the universe is almost fourteen billion years old.

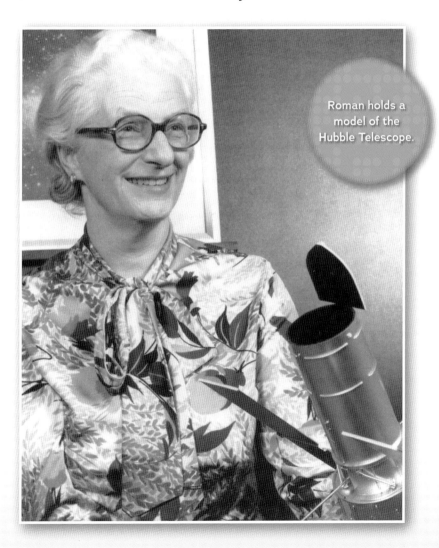

Roman holds a model of the Hubble Telescope.

Roman is recognized for the contributions she's made to science and astronomy. She's known as the Mother of Hubble for her tireless work on the project, which helped take the space telescope from idea to reality. As she predicted, her work at NASA has had a huge influence on astronomy and our understanding of the universe.

TIMELINE

1925

Nancy Grace Roman is born in Nashville, Tennessee.

1942

Roman starts her first year at Swarthmore College.

1949

Roman earns her PhD in astronomy from the University of Chicago and takes her first job in astronomy at the university.

1955

Roman begins working in radio astronomy for the Naval Research Laboratory.

1958

NASA is established by President Dwight D. Eisenhower.

1959

Roman is hired as NASA's first Chief of Astronomy.

1978

Engineers begin designing the Hubble Space Telescope.

1979

Roman retires.

1990

Hubble is launched into space.

2017

Lego decides to immortalize Roman as part of its Women in NASA set.

SOURCE NOTES

6 "Reaching for the Stars," *The Meaning of Swarthmore*, accessed April 10, 2017, http://www.swarthmore.edu/news/meaning/roman.html.

13 "Nancy Grace Roman: Happy 90th Birthday, Nancy!," Women@NASA, accessed March 31, 2017, https://women.nasa.gov/nancy-grace-roman-2/.

19 "The Mother of Hubble," YouTube video, 2:28, posted by "PBS," May 2, 2015, https://www.youtube.com/watch?v=D-ThHmsAmIU.

28 Ibid.

GLOSSARY

astronomer
a scientist that studies stars, planets, galaxies, and other objects in outer space

atmosphere
the mass of air surrounding Earth

constellations
the eighty-eight groupings of stars that form patterns

spectral classification
a system of classifying stars based on the star's spectrum, which provides details about temperature, brightness, and other information

spectrum
the group of colors that a ray of light can be separated into, including the colors seen in a rainbow

stellar astronomy
the study of stars

FURTHER INFORMATION

BOOKS

Nichols, Michelle. *Astronomy Lab for Kids: 52 Family-Friendly Activities.* Beverly, MA: Quarry Books, 2016. Try these hands-on activities to expand your astronomy knowledge.

Rey, H. A. *Find the Constellations.* Rev. ed. Boston: Houghton Mifflin Harcourt, 2016. Study the constellations as Nancy Grace Roman did when she was a kid.

Schwartz, Heather E. *NASA Mathematician Katherine Johnson.* Minneapolis: Lerner Publications, 2018. Learn about another woman who made significant contributions at NASA.

WEBSITES

Astronomy for Kids
http://www.astronomy.com/observing/astro-for-kids
Explore astronomy topics and try fun projects.

Fun with Astronomy
http://www.kidsastronomy.com
Learn all about the universe from our solar system to deep space, and then play space games.

Space
https://kids.usa.gov/science/space/index.shtml
Learn about the solar system, space travel, stars, galaxies, and more.

LERNER

SOURCE

Expand learning beyond the printed book. Download free, complementary educational resources for this book from our website, www.lerneresource.com.

INDEX

ABOUT THE AUTHOR

Heather E. Schwartz has written more than sixty nonfiction books for kids. She always enjoys researching and learning about people with a passion for what they do, like Nancy Grace Roman.